learn to draw

FOREST ANIMALS & WILDLIFE

Learn to draw 20 different woodland animals, step by easy step, shape by simple shape!

Illustrated by Robbin Cuddy • Written by Sandy Phan

© 2012 Quarto Publishing Group USA Inc.
Published by Walter Foster Jr.,
an imprint of Quarto Publishing Group USA Inc.
All rights reserved. Walter Foster Jr. is trademarked.

Associate Publisher: Rebecca J. Razo
Art Director: Shelley Baugh
Senior Editor: Amanda Weston
Associate Editor: Stephanie Meissner
Production Artist: Debbie Aiken, Amanda Tannen
Production Coordinator: Nicole Szawlowski
Production Coordinator: Lawrence Marquez
Production Assistant: Kate Davidson
Illustrated by Robbin Cuddy
Written by Sandy Phan

www.walterfoster.com
6 Orchard Road, Suite 100
Lake Forest, CA 92630

Printed in Shenzhen, China
January 2015
5 7 9 10 8 6
19164

TABLE OF CONTENTS

GETTING STARTED

When you look closely at the drawings in this book, you'll notice that they're made up of basic shapes, such as circles, ovals, and triangles. To draw your favorite creatures, just start with simple shapes as you see here. It's easy and fun!

Circles are the base of this squirrel's body and head.

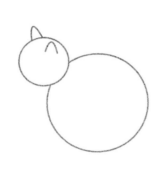 

Ovals are good for drawing a fox's body.

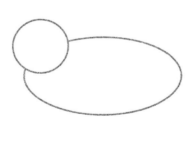 

Triangles are perfect for drawing fins on this trout.

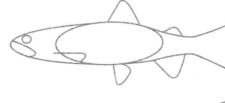 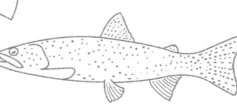

TOOLS & MATERIALS

Before you begin, gather some drawing tools, such as paper, a regular pencil, an eraser, and a pencil sharpener. For color, you can use markers, colored pencils, paint, crayons, or even colored chalk.

eraser

drawing pencil
and paper

sharpener

colored
pencils

felt-tip
markers

paintbrush
and paints

GRIZZLY BEAR

The large brown bear has a hump on its shoulders. It got the name "grizzly," meaning "gray-haired," for its white-tipped fur.

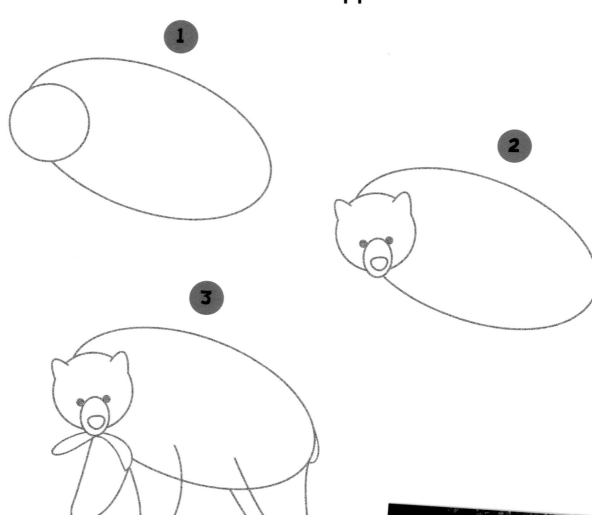

FUN FACT

Grizzly bears hibernate for four to six months!

4

5

AT RISK

Grizzlies used to be common in North America, but are now *endangered,* or in danger of dying off. Only 1,000 to 1,400 remain in the United States because of illegal hunting, human buildings and roads, and loss of the bears' natural food source.

6

GRAY SQUIRREL

Gray squirrels spend most of their time in trees. They use their big, bushy tails for balance, shade, warmth, and swimming.

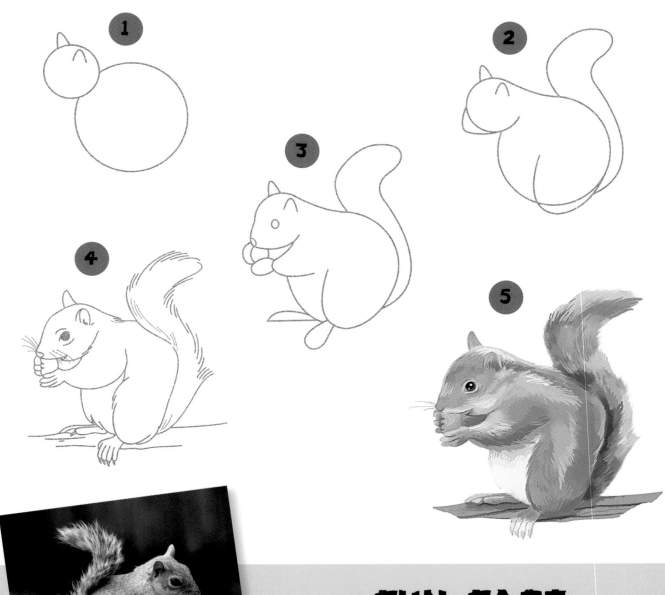

FUN FACT

Squirrels have four front teeth that never stop growing, so they can keep chewing nonstop!

RACCOON

Raccoons are known for the black mask around their eyes, as well as their ringed tails. Watch out, or this masked bandit might make off with your food!

FUN FACT

Raccoons have five fingers on their front feet, so they leave tracks that look like tiny hands. They can do many things, including opening doors, untying knots, or plucking things right out of your pocket!

BARN OWL

This owl has a white, heart-shaped face and its beak looks like the letter "V." It likes to live in barns. That's why it's called a barn owl!

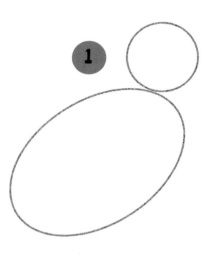

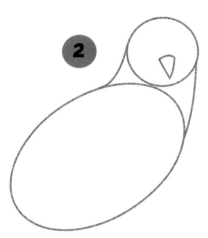

FUN FACT

Barn owls can locate *prey,* or animals they hunt, by sound alone. They also have excellent night vision, and their head can turn 270 degrees. Even prey hiding under plants or snow cannot escape their super senses.

WOLF

The wolf is the largest member of the dog family. Wolves range in color from snowy white to gray, reddish-brown, and all-black.

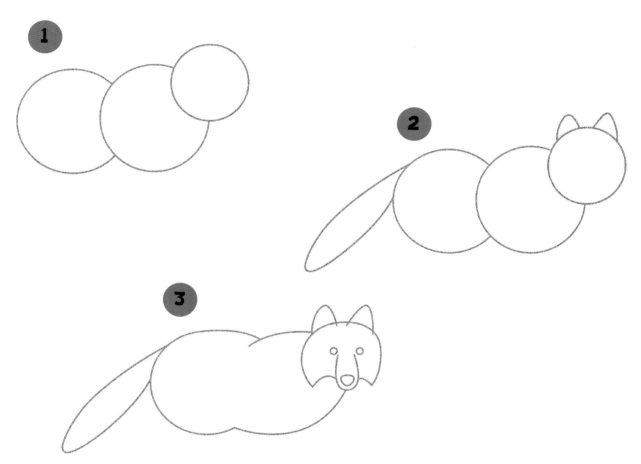

FUN FACT

Young wolf pups love to play. They play hide-and-seek, catch, tag, and wrestling games. Playing helps them learn how to hunt and get along with other wolves.

AT RISK
Wolves almost became *extinct,* or died out, in North America. But their numbers are growing because they have been moved to protected lands.

RED FOX

The red fox has orange-red fur, pointy black ears, and a bushy "brush" tail.

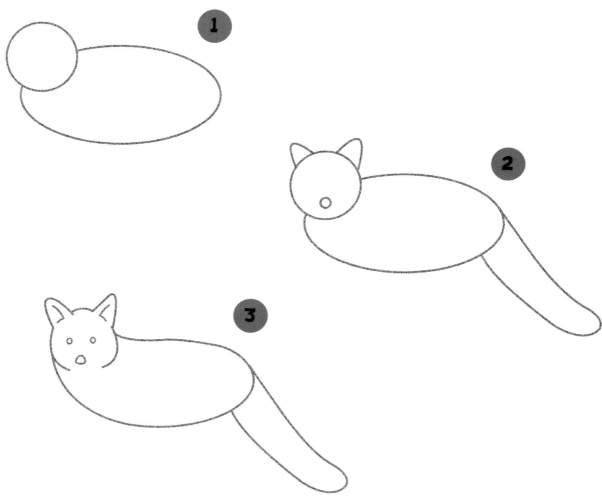

FUN FACT

Red foxes are *omnivores.* This means that they eat many different foods, including fruits, plants, and small animals. Red foxes are good hunters. They are very smart, have a great sense of smell, and pounce on prey like a cat.

MOOSE

Male moose are known for their huge antlers that can grow up to six feet across. Moose have humped shoulders and long faces. A "bell," or flap of skin, hangs from their necks.

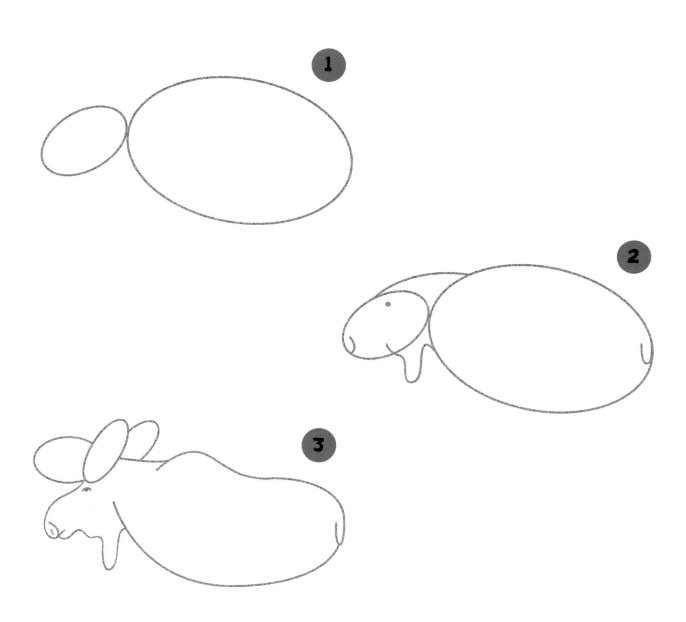

FUN FACT

Moose have four separate areas in their stomachs. They *ruminate,* or re-chew, food that comes back up from the front part of the stomach. A moose stomach can hold up to 100 pounds of food!

CUTTHROAT TROUT

The spotted cutthroat trout gets its name from the red slash on its throat.

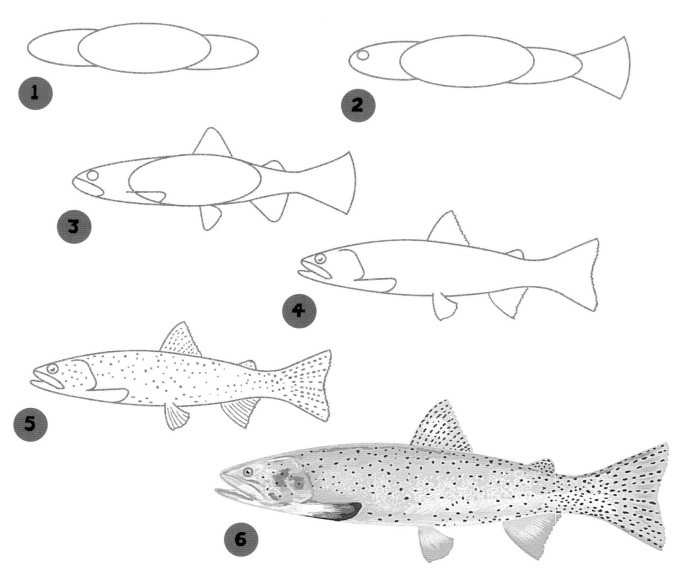

1
2
3
4
5
6

FUN FACT

The cutthroat trout became Wyoming's state fish in 1987. It is the only trout in the state that is *native* to, or originally from, Wyoming.

PRAIRIE RATTLESNAKE

This snake has a rattle on its tail. The diamond shapes on its body help it blend into the ground.

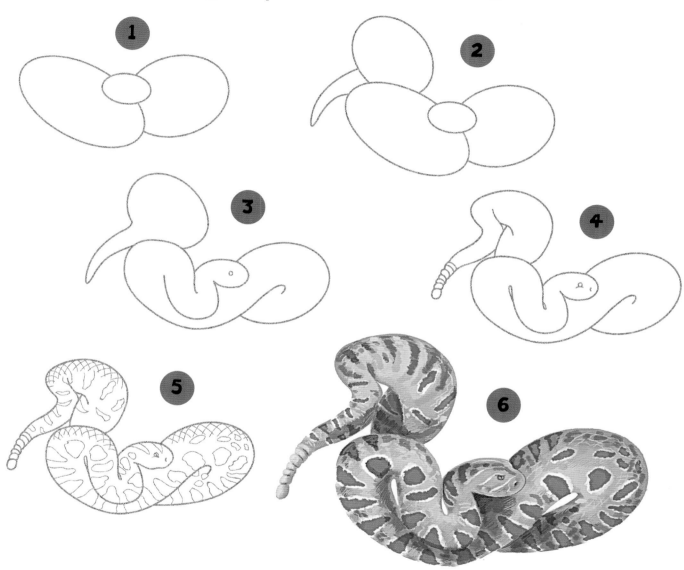

FUN FACT

Rattlesnakes are pit vipers that have hollow spots on the sides of their heads. These pits are organs that can sense heat. They help rattlesnakes hunt warm-blooded prey in the dark.

BIGHORN SHEEP

Male bighorn sheep have large, curved horns. They charge each other with their horns and battle for hours!

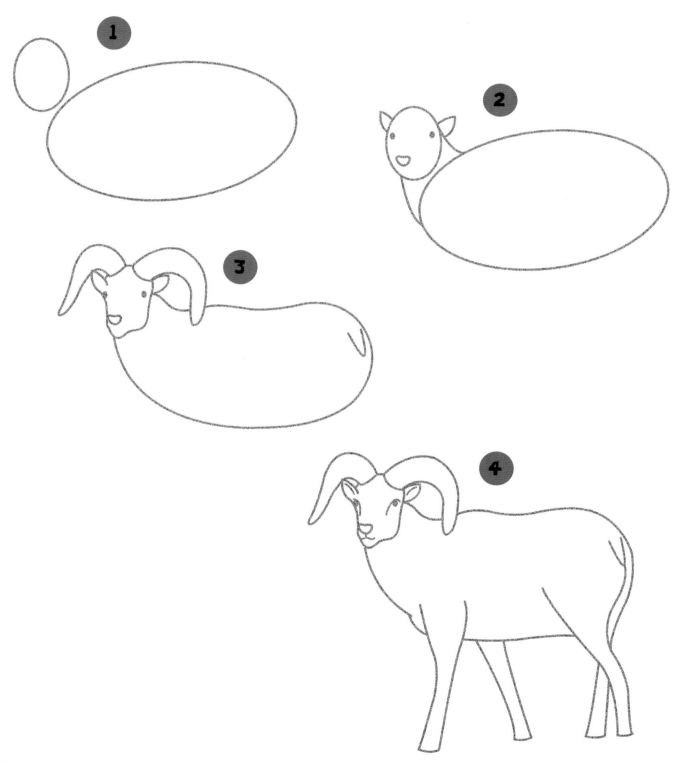

AT RISK

Some desert bighorn sheep are endangered. The plants and water they need to survive are disappearing, because the weather has become hotter and drier where they live.

FUN FACT

Baby bighorn sheep are called lambs. They have soft, woolly coats and little horn buds. At one-day old, a lamb can keep up with its mother when walking and climbing.

BOBCAT

The bobcat is known for its short "bobbed" tail and spiky ear hair. It also has a mane of fur around its face.

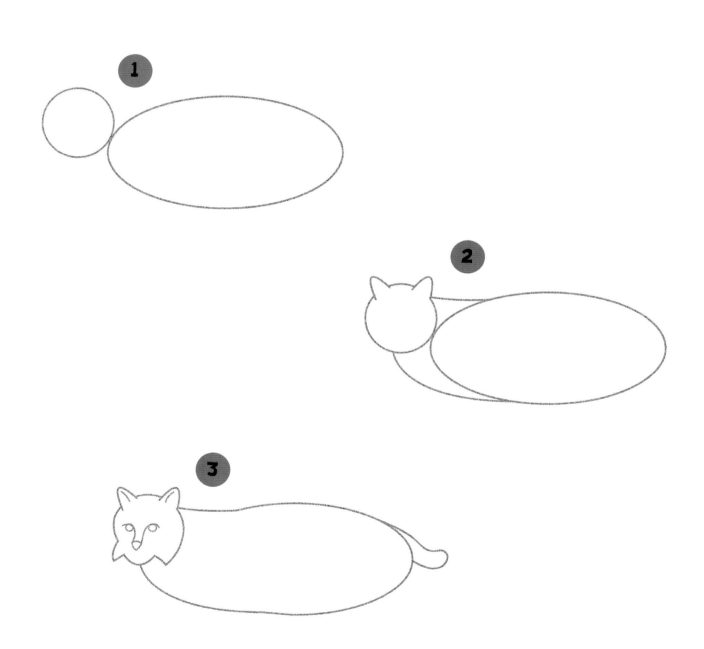

FUN FACT

Also called wildcats, bobcats are about twice as large as their house-cat relatives. They mew, yowl, hiss, and purr, just like domestic cats, but they are fearless hunters that can pounce on much larger animals.

STAG DEER

Male red deer, or stags, have antlers. Their antlers are branched with long, hard, pointy ends.

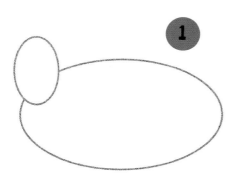

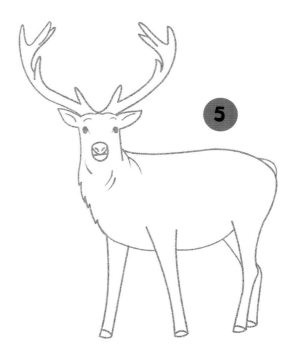

FUN FACT

To compete for female deer, stags have roaring contests. They also walk side by side to see which one is bigger and stronger. Sometimes fights break out, but usually the larger stag with the louder voice wins without even touching his rival.

ROCKY MOUNTAIN GOAT

Rocky Mountain goats have a long beard and two horns that curve backward. Their thick, white fur keeps them warm and helps them blend into the snow.

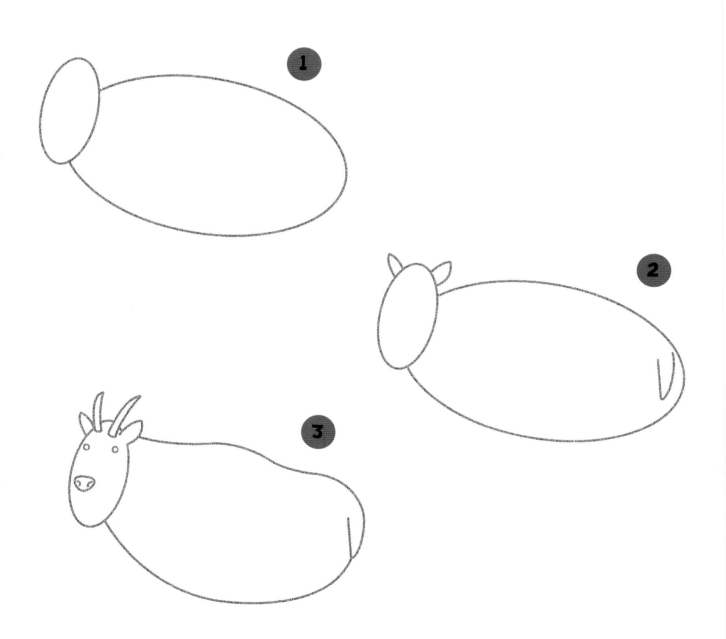

FUN FACT

Rocky Mountain goats can climb icy, rocky cliffs and leap from rock to rock. Their hooves have two toes and rough pads for balance and grip. Few animals—or humans—can reach the Rocky Mountain goat's home high up in the snowy peaks.

bALD EAGLE

The bald eagle has a white head and tail. Instead of flapping its wings, the bald eagle soars through the sky with its brown wings held out almost flat.

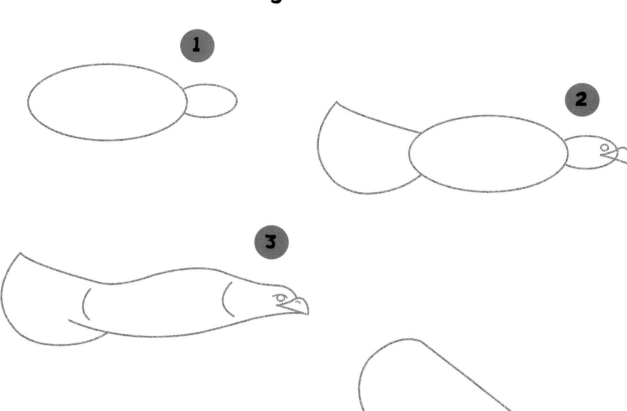

AT RISK

In the mid-1900s, farmers used harmful chemicals called *pesticides* to keep insects from eating their crops. These chemicals leaked into water where bald eagles hunted fish, and the birds became endangered. Fortunately, the government passed laws to control pesticide use, and bald eagle numbers are growing again.

5

6

FUN FACT

The bald eagle is the symbol of the United States. But not all of the founding fathers agreed with this choice—Benjamin Franklin did not want the nation's symbol to be a bird that steals food from other animals! However, he was outvoted, and the bald eagle became the U.S. emblem in 1782. It stands for strength and freedom.

BISON

Bison, also called buffalo, have shaggy brown fur and a large hump on their shoulders. They are known for their long beards and two curved horns.

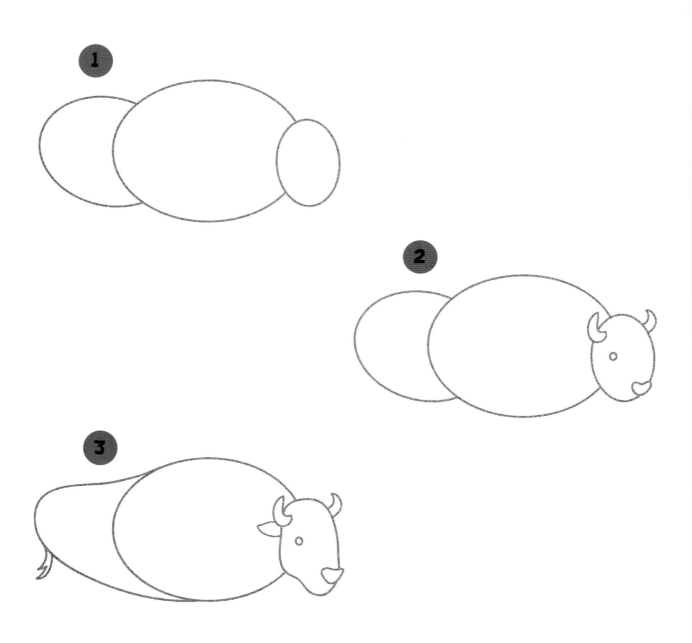

FUN FACT

The American bison's ancestor is the prehistoric long-horned bison. It crossed a land bridge from Asia to North America during the Ice Age with other giant mammals. Millions of bison roamed the Great Plains before hunters killed many of them during the 19th century. Today, only bison with short horns exist, and they are protected by the government.

BEAVER

Beavers have large front teeth, a flat tail, and webbed feet. They tend to be a bit clumsy on land, but they are very graceful in the water.

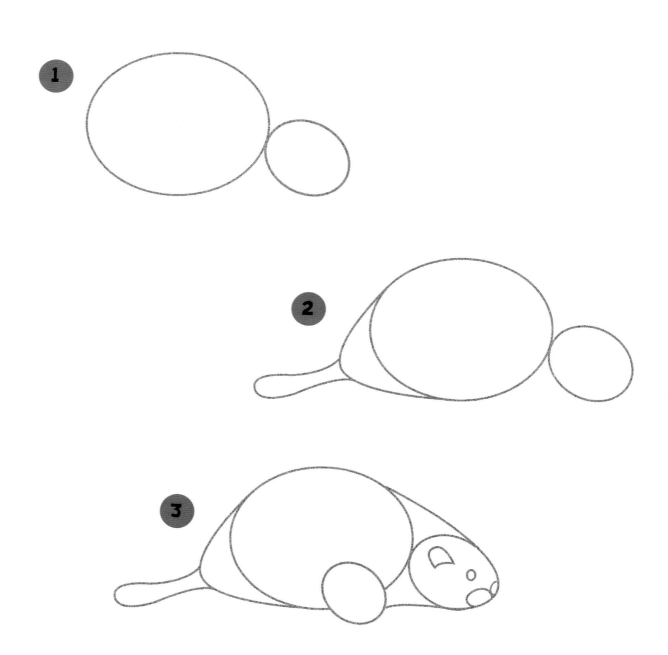

FUN FACT

Beavers can cut down tall trees with their powerful teeth and jaws. They build dams to create large ponds. Then they use mud and branches to build dome-like homes, called lodges, in the middle of the pond. Beaver families get in and out of their lodges through secret, underwater entrances.

COYOTE

The clever coyote is part of the dog family. It is a great swimmer and a fast runner!

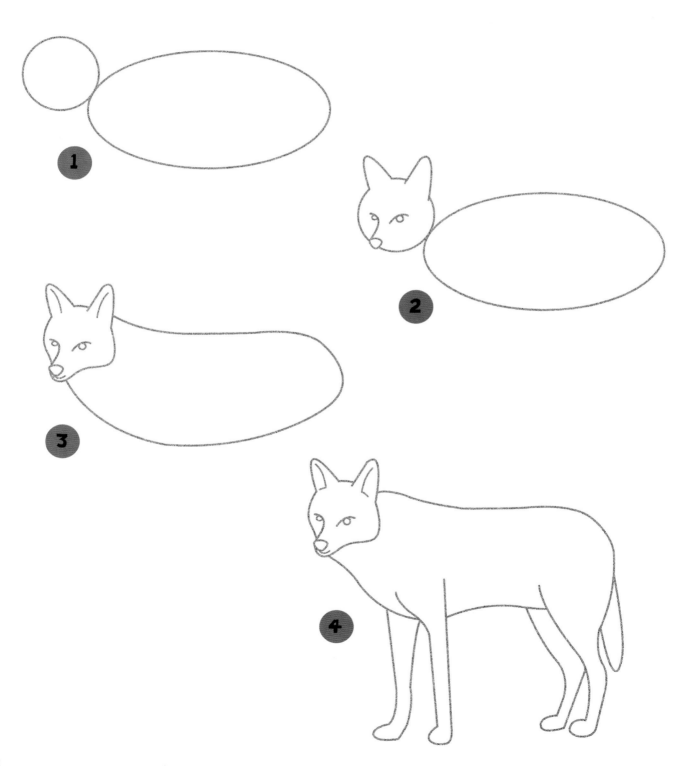

5

6

FUN FACT

Coyotes can be super sneaky and secretive! They often work in pairs or teams to hunt. One coyote may attack an animal from behind while another coyote distracts the prey. Many American Indian groups tell myths and legends about the coyote. It is usually a trickster character in stories that teach lessons about human behavior.

ANTELOPE

Antelope are a group of animals with horns and hooves.
Their horns can be long, short, curved, branched,
or even twisted spirals!

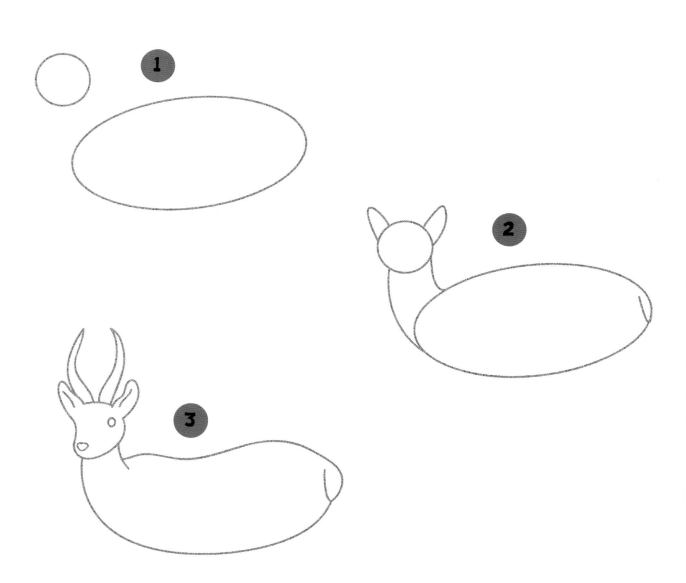

FUN FACT

You may think that antelope are related to deer; however, they are part of an animal family that includes cattle, goats, and sheep. Deer shed their antlers every year, but antelope keep their horns for life.

MOUNTAIN LION

Mountain lions are large wild cats with big paws and sharp claws. Their back legs are bigger than their front legs, so they can jump high and far.

FUN FACT

The mountain lion has many names! It is also called a puma, cougar, panther, and catamount. The name "mountain lion" came from early Spanish explorers to North America who called it *gato monte,* or "cat of the mountain."

MUTE SWAN

The mute swan has a snowy white body and a long, curved neck. It is known for its black face and orange bill.

FUN FACT

Mute swans are not really "mute." They can hiss, snort, and make soft bark-like calls.